A. P. Howard

Carols for Christmas, Easter and Other Festivals

A. P. Howard

Carols for Christmas, Easter and Other Festivals

ISBN/EAN: 9783337379360

Printed in Europe, USA, Canada, Australia, Japan

Cover: Foto ©Thomas Meinert / pixelio.de

More available books at **www.hansebooks.com**

+ GLORY TO GOD +

CAROLS

FOR

CHRISTMAS, EASTER,

AND OTHER FESTIVALS.

BY A. P. HOWARD.

BOSTON:
E. P. DUTTON & COMPANY.
1867.

+ IN THE HIGHEST +

Ralph. Music Typographer

PREFACE.

Most of the following Carols are adapted for either Choir or Sunday School use; but the ones entitled "Wonderful Night," and "A Shepherd Band their Flocks are keeping," are suitable only for Choirs.

The harmony in several of the Carols may seem too difficult for children's music, but our own experience has convinced us that an elaboration of the accompaniment does not trouble children at all, provided the melody is simple and flowing.

When teaching a Carol to children, it will be better, at first, to omit the accompaniment, and play only the melody, until the ear has become familiar with it.

We trust that this little Collection may in a measure supply a deficiency often felt of suitable Christmas and Easter music for Sunday Schools.

A. P. H.

Boston, November, 1866.

INDEX.

"HARK, the glad sound! the Saviour comes!
  The Saviour promised long!
Let every heart prepare a throne,
  And every voice a song.

Our glad hosannas, Prince of Peace,
  Thy welcome shall proclaim;
And heaven's eternal arches ring
  With Thy beloved name."

Carol, Carol, Christians.

A CAROL FOR CHRISTMAS.

Words by Rev. A. C. Coxe, D. D.

Music by A. P. H.

1. Carol, carol, Chris - tians, car - ol joy - ful - ly, Car - ol for the com - ing of
2. Go ye to the for - est, Where the myr - tles grow, Where the pine and lau - rel

Christ's Na - tiv - i - ty. And pray a gladsome Christmas To all good Christian
Bend be - neath the snow. There, gather them for Je - sus, And wreathe them for his

men; Car - ol, car - ol, Chris - tians, for Christmas come a - gain.
shrine; Make his tem - ple glo - rious With the box and pine.

Car - ol, car - ol, Chris - tians, Car - ol joy - ful - ly,

Car - ol for the com - - ing of Christ's na - tiv - i - ty.

3

Wreathe your Christmas garland,
 Where to Christ we pray,
It shall smell like carmel
 On our festal day ;
Libanus and Sharon
 Shall not greener be,
Than our holy chancel,
 On Christ's nativity.

4

Carol, carol, Christians !
 Like the Magi now,
Ye must lade your caskets
 With a grateful vow ;
Ye must have sweet incense,
 Myrrh and finest gold,
At our Christmas altar,
 Humbly to unfold.

5

Sound, O sound the trumpet,
 For our solemn feast,
Gird thine armor, Christian,
 Wear thy surplice, priest ;
Go ye to the altar,
 Pray with fervor, pray,
For Jesus' second coming,
 And the latter day.

6

Give us grace, O Saviour,
 To put off in might,
Deeds and dreams of darkness,
 For the robes of light !
And to live as lowly,
 As Thyself with men,
So to rise in glory,
 When Thou com'st again.

Shout the Glad Tidings.

Solo.

Music by A. P. H.

1. Zi - on the mar - vel - ous sto - ry be telling, The Son of the
2. Tell how He cometh from na - tion to nation, The heart - cheering
3. Mortals your hom - age be grate - ful - ly bringing, And sweet let the

Highest, how low - ly His birth, The bright - est arch - an - gel in
news let the earth e - cho round, How free to the faith - ful He
gladsome ho - san - na a - rise; Ye an - gels! the full hal - le -

glo - ry ex - cell - ing, He stoops to re - deem thee, He reigns up - on earth.
of - fers sal - vation, How His peo - ple with joy ev - er - last - ing are crown'd.
lu - jah be singing; One cho - rus re - sounds thro' the earth and the skies.

CHORUS.
SOPRANO.
Shout the glad ti - dings, Ex - ult - ing - ly sing; Je-
ALTO.
TENOR.
Shout the glad ti - dings, Ex - ult - ing - ly sing; Je-
BASS.
ru - sa - lem tri - umphs, Mes - si - ah is King.
ru - sa - lem tri - umphs, Mes - si - ah is King.

Hark! the Herald Angels Sing.

MODERATO.

A. P. H.

1. Hark, the her-ald an-gels sing, Glo-ry to the new-born King;

Peace on earth, and mer-cy mild, God and sin-ners re-con-ciled.

2.

Christ by highest heaven adored,
Christ, the everlasting Lord;
Late in time, behold him come,
Offspring of the virgin's womb.

3.

Veiled in flesh, the Godhead, see,
Hail th' incarnate Deity;
Pleas'd as man, with man to dwell,
Jesus, now Emmanuel.

4.

Risen with healing in His wings,
Light and life to all He brings;
Hail the Sun of Righteousness,
Hail the heav'n-born Prince of Peace!

CHORUS.

Joy - ful all ye na - tions rise, Join the tri - umph of the skies;

Joy - ful all ye na - tions rise, Join the tri - umph of the skies;

With the an - gel - ic host proclaim, Christ is born in Beth - le - hem.

With the an - gel - ic host proclaim, Christ is born in Beth - le - hem.

Hark, What mean those Holy Voices.

Music by A. P. H.

1. Hark! what mean those ho - ly voi - - ces, Sweet - ly
2. Hear them tell the won - drous sto - - ry, Hear them
3. Christ is born, the great A - noint - ed; Heav'n and
4. Haste, ye mor - tals, to a - dore him, Learn His

sound - ing through the skies? Lo! th' an - gel - ic
chant in hymns of joy.— Glo - ry in the
earth his prais - es sing; Oh, re - ceive whom
name, and taste His joy. Till in heaven ye

host re - joi - ces, Heav'n - ly hal - le - lu - jahs rise.
high - est — Glo - ry! Glo - ry be to God on high!
God ap - point - ed For your Pro - phet, Priest, and King.
sing be - fore Him,— Glo - ry be to God on high!

CHORUS.

Peace on earth, good will from heav'n, Reach-ing far as man is found,

Peace on earth, good will from heav'n, Reach-ing far as man is found,

Souls redeemed and sins for-giv-en, Loud our gol-den harps shall sound.

Souls redeemed and sins for-giv-en, Loud our gol-den harps shall sound.

14

A Shepherd Band their Flocks are Keeping.

[The words of this hymn were written in the latter part of the 16th century.]

May be sung without Accompaniment.   Music by Dr. S. P. Tuckerman.

1. A shep-herd band their flocks are keeping, And gentle lambs are sweetly

2. Glad ti-dings of great joy He bringeth, The azure vault with anthems

3. "To you this day is born a SAVIOUR, Your PROPHET, PRIEST, and KING for-

4. "On earth be peace with mercy blending, Good will to men, and love un-

sleep-ing; When sud-den-ly they all be-hold, An

ring-eth; "IM-MAN-U-EL a-wakes the song, And

ev-er; "All glo-ry be to God," they cry, "All

end-ing;" Thus sweet-ly sing the an-gel throng, And

an - gel   in   bright   robes   with   harp   of   gold.

count - less   hosts   the   glori - ous   theme   pro - long.

glo - ry   be   to   God,"   let   earth   re - ply.

all   the   heaven - ly   host   re - hearse   the   song.

5.

Through field and wood the song resoundeth,
O'er hill and vale the chorus boundeth;
Exultingly the echoes roll,
And hymns of triumph spread from pole to pole.

6.

The shepherds view the host returning,
Their hearts with holy ardor burning;
To Bethlehem they wend their way,
Repeating with glad tongues th' angelic lay.

7.

In haste they seek the heavenly stranger;
They find the Babe laid in a manger;
With wonder and with awe they fall,
And joyfully adore him Lord of all!

8.

Now every voice with rapture swelleth;
For Christ the Lord with mortals dwelleth;
Let men and angels Him adore,
And shout their loud Hosannas evermore.

Wonderful Night.

Music by A. P. H.

May be sung without Accompaniment.

1. Wonderful night! wonderful night! Angels and shining im - mor - tals,

2. Wonderful night! wonderful night! Dreamed of by prophets and sa - ges!

Thronging thine eb - o - ny por - tals, Fling out their banners, their banners of light,
Welcomes Thy hallowing, Thy hallowing might.

Fling out their banners of light,

Manhood redeemed for all a - ges,

Welcomes Thy hallow - ing might,

Won - der - ful night! Ho - ly night! Won - der - ful night! Ho - ly night!

Won - der - ful night! Ho - ly night! Won - der - ful night! Ho - ly night!

3.

Wonderful night!
Down o'er the stars to restore us,
Leading His flame-winged chorus,
Comes the Eternal to sight,
 Wonderful night! holy night!

4.

Wonderful night!
Sweet be thy rest to the weary,
Making the dull heart and dreary,
Laugh in a dream of delight,
 Wonderful night! holy night!

5.

Wonderful night!
Let me as long as life lingers,
Sing with the cherubim singers,
Glory to God in the height,
 Wonderful night! holy night!

Epiphany Carol.

SOLO.   Music by A. P. H.

1. Cold on His cra - dle the dew - drops are shi - ning;
2. Say, shall we yield Him, in cost - ly de - vo - tion,

Low lies His head.... with the beasts of the stall;
O - - dors of E - dom, and offer - rings di - vine,

An - gels a - dore Him, in slum - ber re - clin - ing,
Gems of the moun - tain, and pearls of the o - - cean,

Ma - ker and Mon - arch and Sa - viour of all.—Cho.
Myrrh from the for - - est, or gold from the mine?—Cho.

3.
Vainly we offer each ample oblation,
Vainly with gifts would His favor secure ;
Richer by far is the heart's adoration,
Dearer to God are the prayers of the poor.—Cho.

4.
Brightest and best of the Sons of the morning!
Dawn on our darkness and lend us thine aid ;
Star of the East, the horizon adorning,
Guide where our infant Redeemer is laid.—Cho.

CHORUS.
Soprano.

Bright - est and best of the Sons of the morn - ing, Dawn on our darkness, and

Alto.

Tenor.

Brightest and best of the Sons of the morning, Dawn on our darkness, and

Bass.

lend us Thine aid ; Star   of   the   East,   The ho - ri - zon a-

lend us Thine aid ; Star   of   the   East,   The ho - ri - zon a-

dorn - ing,   Guide where our In - fant Re - deem - er is   laid.

dorn - ing,   Guide where our In - fant Re - deem - er is   laid.

As with gladness Men of Old.

AN EPIPHANY CAROL.

By permission of O. Ditson.

Arranged from Mendelssohn by Dr. S. P. Tuckerman.

1. As with gladness men of old, Did the guid-ing star be - hold;

2. As with joy - ful steps they sped, To that low - ly man - ger bed;
3. As they of - fered gifts most rare, At that man - ger rude and bare;

4. Ho - ly Je - sus, ev - 'ry day, Keep us in the nar - row way;

5. In the heav'n - ly coun - try bright, Need they no cre - a - ted light;

As with joy they hailed its light, Lead - ing on - ward, beaming bright;

There to bend the knee be - fore Him whom heav'n and earth a - dore;
So may we with ho - ly joy, Pure and free from sin's al - loy;

And when earth - ly things are past, Bring our ran - som'd souls at last,

Thou its Light, its Joy, its Crown, Thou its Sun, which goes not down;

AS WITH GLADNESS MEN OF OLD.

So, most gracious Lord, my we   Ev - er more be   led   to Thee.

So may we with will - ing feet,   Ev - er seek Thy mer - cy seat,
All our costli - est trea -sures bring,   Christ, to Thee, our heav'n - ly King.

Where they need no   star   to   guide, Where no clouds Thy glo - ry hide.

There for - ev - er may we sing   Al - le - lu - ias   to our King.

Epiphany Carol.

FOR SUNDAY SCHOOLS.

Music by Dr. S. P. Tuckerman.

1. As with glad - ness men of old,   Did the guid - ing star be - hold;

As with joy they hailed its light, Lead - ing on - ward, beaming bright;

So, most gracious Lord, may we Ev - er more be led to Thee.

2.

As with joyful steps they sped
To that lowly manger bed ;
There to bend the knee before
Him whom heaven and earth adore ;
So may we with willing feet
Ever seek Thy mercy seat.

3.

As they offer'd gifts most rare,
At that manger rude and bare;
So may we with holy joy,
Pure and free from sin's alloy,
All our costliest treasures bring,
Christ, to Thee, our heavenly King.

4.

Holy Jesus, every day
Keep us in the narrow way ;
And when earthly things are past,
Bring our ransomed souls at last,
Where they need no star to guide,
Where no clouds Thy glory hide.

5.

In the heavenly country bright
Need they no created light;
Thou its Light, its Joy, its Crown,
Thou its Sun, which goes not down ;
There forever may we sing
Alleluias to our King.

Jesus Lives! O Day of Days.

A CAROL FOR EASTER.

Words by Rev. Geo. D. Wildes, Rector of Grace Church, Salem.   Music by A. P. H.

1. Je - sus lives! O Day of Days! Glad we bring our grate - ful praise; He is ris - en! Gone the gloom, An - gels sit with - in the tomb. Vain the taunt of Jew de - ny - ing,

Vain the vaunt o'er Je - sus dy - ing. Heaven - ly voi - ces

from the grave, Now pro - claim His pow'r to save.

CHORUS.

Soprano.
He is ris - en! Come and see, How He triumphed migh - ti - ly;

Alto.

Tenor.
He is ris - en! Come and see, How He triumphed migh - ti - ly;

Bass.

Conqueror thus, o'er all His foes, Je - sus from the dead a - rose.

Conqueror thus, o'er all His foes, Je - sus from the dead a - rose.

2.

Lord and Prophet—Spake He not?
Have ye His own word forgot,
Telling while in Galilee,
Thus the victory should be?
How through scorn and dire affliction,
Thorny way and crucifixion,
Vanquished Death, and rent the grave—
Christ, the King, should live to save?
Cнorus.—He is risen! etc.

3.

Tearful, to the Sepulchre
Mary comes in grief and fear;
Sees the stone now rolled away,
Hears the waiting angels say,
" Why the dead among the living
Seek ye?" Lo! the Lord Life-giving

Rises! vain the watch, the grave;
Prince of Life, He lives to save!
Cнorus,—He is risen! etc.

4.

Welcome then, the Day of Days!
Lord, 'tis Thine, our tuneful praise;
Thine, for us, the Tempted, Tried,
Thine, for us, the Crucified;
Thine, for us, the Resurrection,
Thine, the Life, the Sure Protection.
Saviour, Sovereign o'er the grave,
May we know Thy power to save.

Cнorus.

He is risen! joyfully,
Lord! we raise our song to Thee;
Conqueror thus, o'er all His foes,
Jesus from the dead arose.

Easter Bells.

Music by A. P. H.

Soprano.

1. Let the mer - ry church bells ring, Hence with tears and sighing; Frost and cold are

Alto.

2. Let the birds sing out again, From their leafy chapel, Prais - ing Him with

Tenor.

3. Let the tho't of grief be past, This our comfort giv - eth; He was slain on

Bass.

fled from spring, Love hath conquered dying, Flowers are smiling, fields are gay,

whom in vain, Satan sought to grapple, Sounds of joy come fast and thick,

Friday last, But to-day He liveth, Mourning heart must needs be gay,

EASTER BELLS.

Sun - ny is the weath - er, With our ris - ing Lord to-

As the breezes flut - ter, Re - sur - rex - it non est

Nor let sor - row vex it, Since the ve - ry grave can

day, All things rise to - geth - er, Let the merry church bells ring,

hic, Is the strain they ut - - ter, Let the merry church bells ring,

say, Chris - tus re - sur - rex - - it, Let the merry church bells ring,

ring, ring, ring, Let the mer-ry church bells ring, ring, ring, ring.

ring, ring, ring, Let the mer-ry church bells ring, ring, ring, ring.

ring, ring, ring, Let the mer-ry church bells ring, ring, ring, ring.

Now at the Lamb's High Royal Feast.

[May be sung by children without Alto, Tenor and Bass, letting the boys however, sing the phrases marked for them in the Alto.]

Music by A. P. H.

1. Now at the Lamb's high roy-al feast, In robes of saint-ly white we sing,

2. And as th' a-veng-ing an-gel passed, Of old the blood besprinkled door,
3. So Christ our Paschal Sac-ri-fice, Has brought us safe all per-ils through,

4. Hail! purest Vic-tim Heav'n could find, The pow'rs of hell to o-ver-throw,

5. Hail! victor, Christ, hail! ris-en King! To Thee a-lone be-longs the crown,

Through the Red Sea, Through the Red Sea, In safe - ty, in safe - ty

As the cleft sea As the cleft sea, a passage gave, a pas - sage
Has brought us safe, Has bro't us safe, All perils through, all per - ils

Who didst the chains, Who didst the chains, of death de - stroy, of death de-

To Thee a - lone, To Thee a - lone, Belongs the crown, Belongs the

brought, Through the Red Sea, in safety brought, By Jesus, our immor - tal King.

gave, As the cleft sea a passage gave, Then clos'd to whelm th' Egyptians o'er.
through, While for unleav'ned bread we need, But heart sincere and purpose true.

stroy, Who didst the chains of death destroy, Who dost the prize of life be - stow.

crown, Who hast the gates of heav'n unbarred, And dragged the Prince of Darkness down.

Hal - le - lu - jah, hal - le - lu - jah, hal - le - lu - jah, A-

Hal - le - lu - jah, hal - le - lu - jah, hal - le - lu - jah, A-

men, Hal - le - lu - jah, hal - le - lu - jah, hal - le - lu - jah, A - men.

men, Hal - le - lu - jah, hal - le - lu - jah, hal - le - lu - jah, A - men.

Angels, roll the Rock away.

A. P. H.

1. An - gels, roll the rock a - way; Death, yield up thy might - y prey;
2. Shout, ye se - raphs! an - gels, raise, Your e - ter - nal song of praise!
8. Ho - ly Fa - ther, Ho - ly Son, Ho - ly Spi - rit, Three in One!

See, our Sa - viour quits the tomb, Glowing with im - mor - tal bloom.
Let the earth's re - mo - test bound E - cho to the bliss - ful sound.
Glo - ry as of old to Thee, Now and ev - er - more shall be.

CHORUS.

Christ, the Lord, is risen to - day, Sons of men and an - gels say,

Raise your joys and tri - umphs high, Sing, ye heav'ns, and earth re - ply.

Let the Song be Begun.

MELODY.

Music by Dr. S. P. TUCKERMAN.

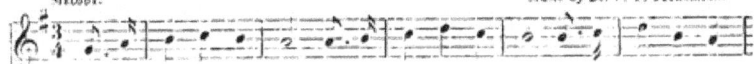

1 Let the song be be - gun, For the bat - tle is done, And the vic - to - ry
2. They that follow'd in pain, Shall now follow to reign, And the crown shall ob-
3. For the foe nev - er more Can approach to the shore, Where the conflict is

won ; And the foe is scatter'd, And the pri - son shatter'd, Sing of joy, Sing of
tain ; They were sore as - saulted, They shall be ex - alt - ed, Sing of rest, Sing of
o'er ; There is joy su - per - nal, There is life e - ternal, Sing of peace, Sing of

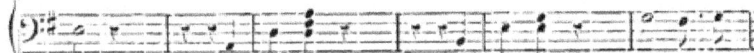

joy, And to-day raise the lay ;—Gloria in ex - cel - sis ! Glo - ria in excel - sis !
rest, And again pour the strain ;—Gloria in ex - cel - sis ! Glo - ria in excel - sis !
peace, Earth and skies bid it rise ;—Gloria in ex - cel - sis ! Glo - ria in excel - sis !

The World itself keeps Easter Day.

MELODY.

Music by Dr. S. P. TUCKERMAN.

1. The world it - self keeps Eas - ter Day, And Eas - ter larks are sing-
2. There stood three Marys by the tomb, On Eas - ter morn - ing ear-

ing, And Eas - ter flow'rs are blooming gay, And Easter buds are spring-
ly, When day had scarcely chas'd the gloom, And dew was white and pear-

ing. The Lord of all things lives anew, And all His works are ri - sing
ly, With lov - ing, but with erring mind, They came the Prince of Life to

too.
find. } Al - le - lu - jah! Al - le - lu - jah! Al - le - lu - jah! Praise the Lord.

3.

But earlier still the Angel sped,
   His words comfort giving ;
" And why" he said, " among the dead,
   Thus seek ye for the living?"
The risen Jesus lives again,
To save the souls of sinful men.
      Allelujah! &c.

4.

The world itself keeps Easter Day,
   And Easter larks are singing:
And Easter flowers are blooming gay,
   And Easter buds are springing;
The Lord is risen, as all things tell,
Good Christians, see ye rise as well.
      Allelujah! &c.

MISCELLANEOUS.

Jesus, Saviour of my Soul.

ARRANGED FOR MALE VOICES.

A German Hymn.
"Müde bin ich geh zur Ruh."

1st Tenor.

1. Je - sus, Sa - viour of my soul, Let me to Thy bo - som fly,

2d Tenor.

2. Hide me, O, my Sa - viour, hide, Till the storm of life is past;
3. Oth - er re - fuge have I none, Hangs my helpless soul on Thee;

1st Bass.

4. All my trust on Thee is stayed, All my help from Thee I bring;

2d Bass.

While the waves of trou - ble roll, While the tem - pest still is high.

Cres. *Dimineuendo.* *Ritard.*

Safe in - to the ha - ven guide, O, re - ceive my soul at last.
Leave, ah, leave me not a - lone, Still sup - port and com - fort me.

Cov - er my de - fence - less head, With the sha - dow of Thy wing.

Jesus, Saviour of my Soul.

ARRANGED FOR MIXED VOICES.

A German Hymn.

1. Je - sus, Sa - viour of my soul, Let me to Thy bo - som fly,

2. Hide me, O, my Sa - viour, hide, Till the storm of life is past;

3. Oth - er re - fuge have I none, Hangs my helpless soul on Thee;

4. All my trust on Thee is stayed, All my help from Thee I bring;

While the waves of trou - ble roll, While the tem - pest still is high.

Safe in - to the ha - ven guide, O, re - ceive my soul at last.

Leave, ah, leave me not a - lone, Still sup - port and com - fort me.

Cov - er my de - fence - less head, With the sha - dow of Thy wing.

They are going, ever going.

Music by A. P. H.

1. They are go-ing, ev-er go-ing, Je-sus called them long a-go, All the
2. They are go-ing, on-ly go-ing, When with summer earth is dressed, In their
3. All a-long the mighty a-ges, All adown the solemn time, They have
4. They are go-ing, on-ly go-ing, Out of pain, and in-to bliss, Out of
5. Lit-tle hearts forev-er stain-less; Lit-tle hands as pure as they; Lit-tle

1 wintry time they're passing, Softly as the falling snow, When the violets in the springtime Catch the
2 cold hands holding roses, Folded to each silent breast; When the autumn hangs red banners, Out a-
3 taken up their homeward march To that serener clime; Where the watching, waiting angels Lead them
4 sad and sinful weakness, In-to perfect holiness; Snowy brows no care shall shade them, Bright eyes
5 feet by angels guided, Ne-ver a for-bidden way! They are going, ev-er going, Leaving

1 a-zure of the sky, They are carried out to slumber, Sweetly where the violets lie.
2 bout the harvest sheaves, They are going, ev-er going, Thick and fast like falling leaves.
3 from the shadows dim To the brightness of His presence, Who has called them unto Him.
4 tears shall never dim them, Rosy lips no time shall fade them, Jesus called them unto Him.
5 many a lone-ly spot, But 'tis Je-sus who has called them, "Suffer and forbid them not."

I'm a Lonely Traveller Here.

Music by A. P. H.

1. I'm a lone-ly trav'ler here, Weary, op-prest, But my journey's
2. I'm a wea-ry trav'ler here, I must go on; For my journey's
3. I'm a trav-'ler to a land Where all is fair; Where is seen no
4. I'm a trav-'ler and I go Where all is fair; Farewell all I've
5. I'm a trav-'ler, call me not, Upward's my way; Yonder is my

end is near, Soon I shall rest: Dark and dreary is the way,
end is near, I must be gone: Brighter joys than earth can give,
bro-ken band, Saints, all are there: Where no tear shall ev-er fall,
loved be-low, I must be there: Worldly hon-ors, hopes and gain,
rest and lot, I can-not stay: Fare-well, earthly pleasures all,

Toil-ing I've come, Ask me not with you to stay, Heav'n is my home.
Win me a-way, Pleasures that for-ev-er live, I can-not stay.
No heart be sad, Where the glo-ry is for all, And all are glad.
All I re-sign; Welcome sor-row, grief, and pain, If heav'n be mine.
Pil-grim I roam, Hail me not, in vain you call, Yonder's my home.

Jerusalem, the Golden.

ALLEGRO.

[Hymn 276 of the Protestant Episcopal Collection.]

Music by A. P. H.

1. Je - ru - sa - lem, the gol - den, With milk and hon - ey blest, Be-
2. They stand, those walls of Zi - on, All ju - bi - lant with song, And

3. There is the throne of Da - vid, And there from care re - leased, The
4. O sweet and blessed coun - try, The home of God's e - lect! O

neath thy con - tem - pla - tion, Sink heart and voice op - prest, I
bright with many an an - gel, And all the mar - tyr throng; The

shout of them that tri - umph, The song of them that feast; And
sweet and bles - sed coun - try, That eag - er hearts ex - pect! Je-

know not, Oh! I know not, What joys a - wait us there, What
Prince is ev - er in them, The day - light is se - rene, The

they who with their Leader, Have conquer'd in the fight, For-
sus in mer - cy bring us To that dear land of rest, Who

ra - dian - cy of glo - ry, What bliss be - yond com - pare.
pas - tures of the bless - ed Are decked with glo - rious sheen.

ev - er, and for - ev - er, Are clad in robes of white.
art with God the Fa - ther, And Spi - rit ev - er blest.

On Jordan's Stormy Banks I Stand.

[Hymn 272.]

Music by A. P. H.

1. On Jor - dan's stor - my banks I stand, And cast a
2. Oh, the trans - port - ing, rap - turous scene, That ri - ses
3. Filled with de - light my rap - tured soul, Can here no

wish - ful eye To Ca - naan's fair and hap - py
to my sight! Sweet fields ar - rayed in liv - ing
lon - ger stay; Though Jor - dan's waves a - round me

land, Where my po - ses - sions lie.
green, And riv - ers of de - light!
roll, Fear - less I'd launch a - way.

Should my Tears Forever Flow.

[From Hymn 139. III. 3.]

Music by A. P. H.

Should my tears for - ev - er flow, Should my zeal no lan - guor know,

Should my tears for - ev - er flow, Should my zeal no lan - guor know,

This for sin could not a - tone, Thou must save, and Thou a - lone;

This for sin could not a - tone, Thou must save, and Thou a - lone;

In my hand no price I bring, Simply to Thy cross I cling.

In my hand no price I bring, Simply to Thy cross I cling

Simply to Thy cross............. I cling.